BEFORE I MADE HISTORY™

Thank You, Squanto!

by Peter and Connie Roop

SCHOLASTIC INC.

New York   Toronto   London   Auckland   Sydney
Mexico City   New Delhi   Hong Kong   Buenos Aires

ISBN 0-439-79254-1

12 11 10 9 8 7   7 8 9 10/0

Printed in the U.S.A.   40
First printing, October 2005

For Cap, Kitty, Pat, and Brad,
who bravely face the world
with smiles on their faces
and warmth in their hearts!

Contents

Introduction

Squanto, a Native American, made history. He was a member of the Patuxet tribe that lived along the shores of Massachusetts. Squanto became famous for helping the Pilgrims survive. Squanto also helped the Pilgrims celebrate their first harvest festival in America.

The Pilgrims called him Squanto. Do you know that Squanto's real name was Tisquantum?

Squanto grew up learning how to live as a Wampanoag. Do you know that he used these skills to help the Pilgrims?

Squanto grew up tall and strong. Do you know that as a boy he liked to play a rough, tough ball game on the beach?

Squanto learned how to survive in the woods on his own. Do you know he had to spend a winter alone before he could become a full member of his tribe?

Squanto lived close to the shore. Do you know an English sea captain kidnapped him and took him to England?

Squanto learned by watching and listening. Do you know that he learned to speak English?

Squanto returned to his home after nine years in England. Do you know he was kidnapped again and taken to Spain this time?

Squanto came home again. Do you know that when he returned none of his Patuxet people were alive?

Squanto was sent by Massasoit, the chief of the Wampanoag, to talk with the Pilgrims. Do you know Squanto helped make a protective treaty between the Native Americans and the Pilgrims that lasted forty years?

Squanto celebrated the Pilgrims' first harvest festival in America. Do you know that Squanto's people celebrated their harvest festival with a feast and by giving thanks every year, too?

The answers to these questions lie in who Squanto was as a boy and as a young man. This book is about Squanto before he made history.

1
Squanto Is Born

The summer sun rose over Patuxet Bay. Its warm rays fell on a small *wetu*, or wigwam. The *wetu* was on a hilltop near the shore. A stream ran along the bottom of the hill.

A baby cried inside the *wetu*. The baby's mother rocked him to sleep. She wondered if he would grow up to be a good hunter who would provide meat for his family.

The baby's father smiled at his infant son. He wondered if the boy would grow up to be a *pniese*, a leader who would help his people.

The proud parents named their son Tisquantum. Today we know him as Squanto. This is what the Pilgrims called him, because they couldn't pronounce his real name.

While Squanto slept, his parents went

outside. They looked around their summer home. Squanto's parents were happy they had a healthy son. They were glad Squanto was born into the Patuxet tribe. They were pleased the Patuxets were part of the Wampanoag people, the People of the Dawn.

There were sixty-seven Wampanoag villages. Massasoit was their leader. The villages traded with one another. They held feasts together. In war, they fought together against their enemies. Massasoit made sure that the Wampanoag villages stayed friendly with one another.

Squanto's mother went inside her *wetu*. She gently picked up Squanto. She put Squanto into a wooden cradleboard, a flat wooden baby carrier she used to keep her baby with her while she worked. She picked up the cradleboard and went outside to cook breakfast.

Squanto's mother placed Squanto against the *wetu*'s wall. Squanto watched his mother put sticks into a fire. She hung a clay pot of fish stew to cook over the fire. As the stew steamed, Squanto cried. His mother picked him up. She softly sang him a lullaby and he fell asleep.

Squanto's parents ate the delicious stew out of wooden bowls his father had carved. After breakfast, Squanto's father prepared to go fishing. He would bring fish home for his family to eat.

Squanto's mother took her son back into the *wetu*. She rolled up the sleeping mats and put the bearskin blankets away. She checked her corn basket to see how much corn was left. The summer crop of corn would not be ready for picking until another full moon passed. She decided she had enough corn to make corncakes for dinner that night. They would taste good with the fish her husband would bring home.

Squanto's mother put her son's cradle-board onto her back. She carried Squanto as she gathered blueberries and blackberries. Squanto enjoyed the world as he rode on his mother's back. He watched white clouds sail across the blue sky. He heard seagulls

calling. He listened to waves breaking on the shore. He felt a cool ocean breeze.

Before the sun was straight overhead, his mother's two birchbark baskets were full of berries. They would eat some of the berries that day. Squanto's mother would dry the rest of the berries in the hot summer sun. They would enjoy the dried berries during the long, cold winter.

That night, as Squanto and his parents slept, the moon rose over Patuxet Bay. Another day of Squanto's life was over.

Squanto was probably born about 1590. No one knows the exact date. But we do know Squanto grew up to become the most famous member of the Patuxet tribe.

2
Squanto Grows Up

Each day, Squanto's mother worked in her garden. She put Squanto in the shade of an oak tree. She pulled weeds away from her squash plants. She ran her fingers over the long ears of corn. She picked a few green beans for the evening meal. She was pleased with her crops.

She smiled when she thought of the Green Corn Dance after the harvest. She would celebrate Squanto's birth with her friends and family when they gathered for the festival. There would be food roasted over big fires. There would be dances and games. Squanto would see his first Green Corn Dance. He would hear his people give thanks to *Kiehtan,* the Great Creator.

When Squanto and his mother returned to

the *wetu* that afternoon, they were pleased to see his father. He held up a fine, fat turkey.

Squanto's mother took the turkey. She plucked off the feathers. She saved some of the feathers for Squanto's father to use on his arrows. She roasted the turkey over her fire.

Squanto's father held out the arrow he used to hunt the turkey. Squanto wrapped his little fingers around the arrow. His father smiled. Maybe Squanto would indeed be a hunter when he grew up.

Before he became a hunter, a warrior, or a leader, however, Squanto had to learn the ways of the Patuxet people.

Squanto would be taught like the other Patuxet boys. Since there was no formal school, Squanto would learn from the world around him.

When he was little, Squanto learned by watching his parents. He watched his mother gather dry firewood. From her, he learned the art of starting a fire. He learned how to use a sharp stone knife to skin a rabbit for its meat and fur.

In the summer, Squanto went with his mother to their field. He watched her plant corn. First she made a mound of earth. Then she dug a hole in the mound with a clamshell hoe and dropped in three fish. Next she put four kernels of corn in the hole. Squanto learned that the fish made the plants grow better. Each mound was three feet away from the next mound. When the corn began to grow, his mother would add bean seeds to each mound. She planted squash seeds at the base of each mound and sunflowers between them.

When the corn was harvested, Squanto's mother dried much of it. She dug holes, which she lined with stones. She put the dried corn in woven baskets and then placed them in the holes and covered them with bark and earth. In the winter, she would uncover the corn so they could have corn to eat.

Squanto knew that planting and harvesting was the work of the Patuxet women and girls. By watching his mother, however, Squanto learned how to plant corn, beans, and squash. One day, he would need this valuable skill.

Squanto saw his mother chase hungry crows away from their corn. If the crows ate the corn, Squanto knew he would be hungry in the winter. When he was old enough, Squanto chased the crows, too.

Squanto watched his father make sharp-tipped arrows. He saw him search for and cut the correct branches for the arrows and put feathers on one end. He watched him chip stone to make arrowheads.

One day, his father gave Squanto a toy bow. Squanto practiced until he shot straight. When he was old enough, his father gave Squanto a strong bow and real arrows. His father taught Squanto how to slip silently through the woods. He pointed out deer, bear, fox, raccoon, and wolf tracks. He smiled proudly when Squanto brought home his first deer.

3
Squanto's World

In the fall, Squanto and his family moved from their summer *wetu* to their winter home. They moved away from the bay and into the forest. There they were sheltered from the fierce winter winds. They joined the rest of the Patuxet people in their winter longhouses. Many fires burned in the bark-covered longhouses to keep *missittopu*, the great frost, away.

Squanto's family shared the longhouse with five other families. Each family had their own area where they slept and cooked.

Squanto and his parents slept on platforms above the ground. Animal skins kept them warm. His family's buckskin bags and birchbark boxes were stored under the sleeping platforms. His father's weapons hung nearby.

During the winter nights, Squanto listened to his people's stories. He learned how Moshup the giant made an island in the ocean. He knew Moshup was a friend to all the Wampanoag people. Squanto heard that the thick gray fog blowing in from the ocean was smoke from Moshup's pipe. He learned about *Kiehtan*, the Great Creator.

Squanto also heard stories of brave hunters who tracked deer, bear, and even the mighty moose. He listened as men told tales of hunting whales. Squanto learned about the other villages and tribes that lived near the Patuxets.

And Squanto heard tales of the strange white *wautaconuoag*, the coat-men who came from far away across the ocean in great canoes with white wings.

Squanto grew straight and tall. He became a skilled hunter. He speared fish swimming in the streams and ponds near his home. He fished from his dugout canoe. He made eels wiggle out of the mud and caught them. The eels were a special meal for his family.

Squanto grew strong. He raced his friends along the sandy beaches. He swam swiftly across ponds and dove into the ocean. He paddled his dugout with skill and strength.

Squanto often played a ball game on the beach. Two goals were set up far apart. Each team tried to get a small, hard ball past the goal. The boys crashed into one another. They knocked one another down. They scrambled to score the winning goal. The game was rough, but it made the boys tough.

Squanto grew in other ways, too. He was kind to the older members of his tribe and patient with younger boys who looked up to him. Squanto watched, listened, and learned just as a *pniese*, a leader, did.

One spring, when he was about twelve, Squanto took part in a coming-of-age activity. Squanto was blindfolded and led deep

into the forest. He carried a stone hatchet, his bow and arrows, and a stone knife. Squanto had to prepare to survive the winter on his own.

Squanto built his own small *wetu*. He bent poles to make the rounded shape. He peeled bark off trees to cover the poles. He made a hole facing east toward the rising sun for his door. Squanto left a small smoke hole in the roof. He built a fireplace in the center of his *wetu* and started a fire to cook his food and to warm his *wetu*.

Squanto went hunting and shot a deer. He used the skin for his blanket. Squanto used the next deerskin for a door covering. He made snowshoes. During the winter nights, he repaired his weapons and chipped new arrowheads.

When spring returned, men from his village looked for Squanto. When they found him, Squanto was no longer considered a boy but a man of the Patuxet tribe.

4
Kidnapped!

Squanto's life along the shores of Patuxet Bay was good. He had his family and his community. He had the skills of a hunter and a warrior. He was growing into a man respected by his people. He was welcomed in every Wampanoag village.

But the lives of the Wampanoag people living in New England were changing. Each year, more explorers from Europe landed on their shores.

Squanto had heard about the explorers, the *wautaconuoag,* or coat-men. Since the early 1500s, European explorers had sailed along the coast of New England.

In 1607, Captain George Weymouth from

England reached Maine and Massachusetts. His ship was called the *Archangel*. Captain Weymouth and his men were looking for gold. They were also looking for a way around America so they could sail to China.

Captain Weymouth traded knives, hatchets, blankets, and kettles for fox, wolf, deer, beaver, and bear furs.

Captain Weymouth thought folks in England would enjoy seeing native people. He knew the Native Americans would not be willing to sail far from their homes. Captain Weymouth played a trick. He invited some Native American men aboard his ship. Squanto was one of the men.

Squanto was amazed as he gazed around the ship. The masts towered high into the sky like pine trees. The great sails were made of canvas, a material he hadn't seen before. Ropes, large and small, were everywhere. Squanto saw things made from iron, copper, and brass.

Squanto and his companions were invited belowdecks for a meal. While Squanto and

his friends were staring around this strange new world, they were locked into a room.

Soon, Squanto heard waves splashing against the ship's sides. He could tell they were sailing away from shore. Squanto didn't know where he was going. But he knew he had been kidnapped!

When the ship was far from shore, Squanto and his fellow captives were called before Captain Weymouth. Through sign language, and a few French and English words, Captain Weymouth told them he was taking them to England. If Squanto and his companions agreed not to try to escape, they could move freely around the ship. Looking over at the wide ocean, the Native Americans agreed not to escape.

Squanto was frightened and very homesick. He wondered if he would ever go back to the Patuxet. And he wondered what life would be like for him in England.

Just as he had watched his parents as he was growing up, Squanto watched the sailors do their jobs. He listened as they talked.

Word by word, Squanto began learning English.

After two months, the *Archangel* finally sailed into the harbor at Plymouth, England. The docks were busy with men unloading and loading ships. Everywhere there were barrels, crates, and boxes. Goats, cows, horses, and pigs were being put aboard ships sailing to other countries. Sailors shouted their good-byes to loved ones onshore. Others sang songs as they lifted things onto the ships.

The great castle of Sir Ferdinando Gorges guarded bustling Plymouth. Homes and shops climbed the hills.

Squanto stepped onto the shores of England for the first time.

5
Squanto Lives in England

Squanto was a stranger in a strange land. There were more people in England than in all of the sixty-seven Wampanoag villages. The streets of Plymouth were crowded and noisy.

There were many things that were different from the life he knew. Horses pulled carts and carriages. The Patuxets had no horses or wheels. The English sold rabbits, chickens, pigs, ducks, and geese. Squanto and his father had hunted for his family's meat. Some of the English sold fruits and vegetables. Squanto's mother grew their corn, beans, and squash. She picked their cranberries, blueberries, and blackberries.

Squanto saw people selling iron knives and axes. Squanto had made his tools from stone. The English had metal pots, pans, and kettles. The Patuxets made their containers from clay, bark, or woven grass. Squanto had lived in his family's *wetu* and in a longhouse made of poles and bark. The English homes were made out of wood, stone, or brick. Smoke rose from chimneys, not smoke holes.

Everywhere Squanto turned, there was something new to look at. And Squanto was looked at, too. Crowds of people followed Squanto and his companions as they walked through the noisy streets. The people of Plymouth had never seen Native Americans before. They stared in wonder at the Native Americans dressed in deerskin clothes. They looked at the Native Americans' long black hair. They wondered why the Native Americans did not grow beards or wear hats. They stared at their buckskin moccasins.

One day, Squanto and his companions met Sir Ferdinando Gorges. Sir Gorges was an important man in Plymouth. He wanted to settle a colony in New England. He wanted to learn where the best land was. He wanted to learn where the best harbors were. He wanted to know what people lived in the region and what they had to trade.

Squanto watched Sir Gorges make marks on smooth white paper. The paper reminded Squanto of the white birchbark at home. Sir Gorges called the marks he made "writing." When he looked at the marks on the paper and spoke the words, he was "reading." Squanto added these two new words to the English words he already knew.

Squanto began living with Sir Gorges, and there he learned how to eat with a knife, fork, and spoon. He wore English shirts, pants, and coats. He wore a hat and shoes. Squanto also learned many more English words.

But Sir Gorge's dream of settling people in New England ran into trouble. And he ran out of money. He let many of his servants go. Squanto, however, stayed with him, for he had no other place to go. He worked in the garden. Squanto knew how to grow plants from watching his mother. He cared for Sir Gorges's horses. He ran errands.

All the while Squanto dreamed of returning home. And he learned more English.

Several ships set sail from Plymouth for New England. They sailed with high hopes to settle in America. But Squanto wasn't allowed to go with them. Instead, he went to live with a farm family in the English countryside. He plowed with an iron plow instead of the clamshell hoe his mother used. He took care of sheep and cattle instead of hunting and fishing. He drove a horse and cart instead of walking from village to village.

One day, Squanto heard that Captain John Smith was taking two ships to New England. After saying, "*Wunniook*. Be well," to the farm family, Squanto walked to the harbor where Captain Smith's ships were docked.

Squanto met a man named Thomas Dermer who worked on one of Captain Smith's ships. The two men talked and quickly came to an agreement. Dermer told Squanto he would ask Captain Smith if he could sail with them to America. Dermer felt that Squanto could help guide the ships when they were near the American shores. Captain Smith agreed to the plan.

6
Kidnapped Again!

The two ships set sail on March 3, 1614. Squanto sailed on Captain Smith's ship. Dermer sailed on the other ship. Thomas Hunt was captain of this ship.

Squanto was about twenty-four years old when he sailed back to his Patuxet home. They reached America in about six weeks. Before long, Captain Smith said good-bye to Squanto and had him row to shore near his home.

Squanto was very excited to be home at last. He had been away for nine long years, but little seemed to have changed. Green corn grew in the fields. Smoke rose from the *wetus*. Boys chased one another pretending to be young hunters. Girls helped their mothers cook or worked in the gardens.

Squanto was eagerly greeted by his family and friends. They asked him many questions about what had happened to him. At first, it was hard to answer in his people's language, for he had not spoken it in years. But, before long, the words flooded out of him as he described his life in England.

Squanto was glad to be home in the fields and forests of the Wampanoag lands. He hoped never to leave home again. This was where he belonged. Squanto was Patuxet.

One day, an English ship sailed to the shore near the Patuxet village. Squanto knew it could not be Captain Smith's ship. Captain Smith had sailed back to England. Squanto recognized the ship. It was the other ship, the one sailed by Captain Thomas Hunt.

Squanto and twenty men were invited aboard the ship. Captain Hunt said he wanted to trade for beaver pelts and deerskins. He promised the Native Americans a wonderful feast. Squanto might have remembered when he had been tricked by Captain Weymouth years before. He might have thought about being taken to England against his will.

But he knew Captain Hunt already. He had seemed friendly before. And at first, Captain Hunt was friendly to Squanto and his friends. He showed them around his ship. Squanto pointed things out to his friends, naming them in English.

Captain Hunt told the Native Americans he would show them how the great canvas sails were raised. He gave a signal to his sailors. The Native Americans watched the sails rising up the mast. They didn't see the sailors with guns until it was too late. The ship was sailing away from shore.

Squanto was kidnapped again!

Captain Hunt had Squanto and his companions locked in a small room belowdecks. There they spent many miserable days sailing across the Atlantic Ocean. Squanto wondered if he was being taken back to England and what would happen to him.

Captain Hunt knew Captain Smith would

be angry if he returned to England with captured Native Americans. His plan was to sell Squanto and his friends in a different country, then sail home to England.

Captain Hunt wanted the Native Americans to look good when he sold them. He let them come up on deck to wash and to be in the sun. He fed them so they would be healthy. Captain Hunt didn't care about their welfare, he just wanted to make the most money he could from selling Squanto and his companions.

Finally, the ship reached land. Squanto was surprised. The weather was warm. He never remembered weather this warm in England. The houses looked different, too. They had roofs covered with red tiles. Onshore he noticed that people dressed differently than the English. And they spoke a different language.

Squanto had not been returned to England. Instead, he was in Málaga, Spain.

7
Squanto Returns Home

Captain Hunt had chains put on Squanto and his friends. He marched the Native Americans to the slave market. They stood in a line as Spanish men looked at them. They had come to buy the Native Americans as slaves for their farms, homes, and shops.

Then a man wearing a brown wool hood stepped up to Captain Hunt. He was a Spanish priest. He and his fellow priests did not approve of slavery. He offered to buy the Native Americans for a good price. Captain Hunt agreed and took the money. The priests took the chains off Squanto and the others and brought them to their home.

Squanto lived with the priests for three years. As always, he watched and learned.

Before long, he knew words in Spanish. He used his farming skills to help the priests with their crops. He cared for their horses and mules. But Squanto still dreamed of returning to his Patuxet home.

Squanto learned that no Spanish ships sailed to New England. Instead, they sailed much farther south to Florida, Mexico, or South America. Squanto realized he would have to get to England again if he wanted to sail home.

He told his problem to his Spanish friends. They agreed to help him get to England. In 1618, when he was about twenty-eight years old, Squanto set foot in England for the second time.

In 1619, Squanto was able to board a ship sailing to New England. Much to his surprise, Thomas Dermer was onboard!

The two men, one Patuxet and one English, talked about their love for America. Dermer told Squanto about his adventures in Canada. Squanto told Dermer about the tragedy of being kidnapped again. He told him about living in Spain and returning to England.

Both men were eager to go back to New England. Dermer, however, told Squanto that trouble had broken out between some Native Americans and the English. There had been fights. The Native Americans didn't want the English landing unless they came in peace.

Dermer told Squanto he hoped he could talk with his people. He hoped he would tell the Wampanoags that he came in peace. He only wanted to trade as they had done in the old days. Squanto agreed to help his English acquaintance.

The voyage seemed long to Squanto. He wanted the great sails to soar home like a giant bird. After many weeks, the ship reached America in May. They were in Maine, but at least they were in America. Dermer told Squanto he would make sure they continued on to his home on Patuxet Bay.

Finally, the ship landed where the Patuxets lived. Squanto went onshore alone. But he was puzzled. Where was the smoke rising from his people's fires? Where were the shouts of the children playing? Where were the fields of growing corn?

Squanto climbed the hill where the Patuxet *wetus* had stood. All he saw were crumbling piles of bark and rotting poles. There was no one left in his village.

Squanto wondered where his people had gone. Had enemies forced them from their lands? Had they all gone to live with the other Wampanoag tribes? Had the English driven them away from their homes?

Squanto set out to find Massasoit. He would certainly know what happened to the Patuxets.

Squanto reached Pokanoket, Massasoit's village, the next day. He was glad to see the fields of corn, beans, and squash growing under the summer sun. He was pleased to see the many *wetus*. He was happy to see men, women, and children doing everyday things.

8
Squanto, the Last
of the Patuxets

Massasoit invited Squanto into his large *wetu*. He asked Squanto to tell his tale. Squanto told the chief about sailing to Spain. He told him about almost being made a slave. He told Massasoit about returning to England and then coming home.

Then Squanto asked where his people were.

Massasoit told him the terrible news. He said that at about the same time Squanto had been kidnapped, a strange thing had happened. An unknown illness had struck Native Americans along the coast. None of their medicines could cure the disease. Many people, including half of the Wampanoags, had died. The tribes were weakened because so many Wampanoag people were dead. Massasoit feared stronger enemies might invade them now.

Then Massasoit told Squanto the worst news of all. He sadly said that the deadly disease had killed almost every Patuxet. Those who had survived had moved to other villages.

Massasoit explained to Squanto that he no longer trusted the English. He was angry that Captain Hunt had kidnapped more than twenty of his warriors. He was angry about the times when some English had attacked his people. No Englishman would be allowed to set foot on Wampanoag lands.

Squanto lived in Massasoit's village for a while. But he missed his parents and his Patuxet friends.

Massasoit was glad to have Squanto in his village. Squanto was now a *pniese*, a wise leader. He could give advice to Massasoit. He could help defend the village. And if more English came, Squanto could talk to them.

He could help them understand why the Wampanoags were not willing to meet the English or trade with them.

Squanto understood what would happen if Massasoit's enemies attacked the Wampanoags. He hoped maybe the English could help the Wampanoags against their more powerful enemies. He would have to convince Massasoit, however.

In November 1620, an English ship sailed into Patuxet Bay. The ship had a large white flower painted on it. Squanto might have recognized this English flower called the *Mayflower*.

The Wampanoags watched from the forest as the English explored the land. They would leave the *Mayflower* out in the bay and come to shore in a small sailboat.

The English stopped in several places. They acted as if they were looking for something. They sipped water from streams and ponds. Some men hunted with guns in the woods for deer and turkeys. Others looked at the soil, the trees, and the plants.

Some of the English found places where the Wampanoags had stored corn for the winter. Often they stole the corn. This angered the Wampanoags. But they knew their bows and arrows could not stand up to the power of the English guns. All the Wampanoags could do was watch and wait.

Before long, the Wampanoags realized that these English were different from other Englishmen. They had not come to trade for furs. The Wampanoags wondered why these Englishmen had come to America.

One December day, the English came upon the hill where Squanto's Patuxet village had stood. The English liked the small bay at the bottom of the hill. They liked the clear stream running nearby. And they especially liked the open spaces where the Patuxets once grew their corn. They knew this would be a good place for them to grow their crops, too. They wouldn't have to cut down the forest to clear the land. And there were no Wampanoag living there to stop them from settling.

The winter weather was cold and stormy. The *Mayflower* rocked in the bay. When the weather got better, men, women, and children came onshore. English explorers had not brought women and children before. The Wampanoags knew now that the English had come to settle on their land.

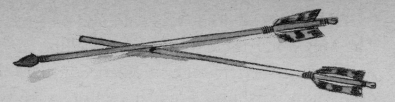

9
Squanto Meets the Pilgrims

Some Englishmen stayed onshore and cut trees to build homes. Others cut tall marsh grass to make thatch for the roofs. The English finished one large building. Here they would store their supplies. Then, in the bitter winter winds, they built two rows of houses along a street.

Massasoit and his warriors watched the English all winter. Squanto talked with Massasoit. He wanted his chief to accept the English settlers. Massasoit, however, still didn't trust the English.

The Wampanoags kept an eye on the

English. Sometimes, a dozen warriors would watch from a distance. Other times, only one or two Wampanoags looked at the settlers. The English were on guard. They didn't know if their relationship with the Native Americans would be friendly or not.

One day in March 1621, a Native American named Samoset came to Massasoit's village. Samoset did not belong to the Wampanoag people. He lived north along the coast. His people were the Pemaquids. But Samoset and Massasoit had long been friends. Squanto and Samoset knew each other, too. They had met before, when Squanto had been in Maine.

Samoset asked Massasoit if he could go talk with the English settlers. Massasoit agreed, for he knew that Samoset spoke a little English he had learned from traders.

On March 16, 1621, Samoset bravely walked alone into the English village. Samoset carried a bow and two arrows in his hand but no other weapons. The English were alarmed at his behavior. They wondered why he boldly came to see them when no other Native Americans had come before.

The settlers were very surprised when Samoset said to them in English, "Welcome, English." Samoset held out the two arrows. One had an arrowhead, which meant war. The second arrow had no arrowhead. This meant peace. Samoset offered the English the arrow without a point. They understood he had come in peace.

A strong wind blew. Samoset was dressed only in his moccasins and a leather breechcloth around his waist. The English gave him a coat to wear. They gave him biscuits, cheese, butter, pudding, and some duck to eat. Samoset was very pleased.

He told the English settlers that the land they had chosen was called Patuxet after the people who had once lived there. He explained how most of the Patuxet had died from a disease. He told them other things about the people and the land. He told them that

Massasoit and his Wampanoag people were angry at the English. Samoset spent the night in one of the English homes. The next morning, Samoset told the settlers that he was leaving. He said he would be back the next day with someone who spoke much better English than he did.

In the morning, Samoset and Squanto went to the English village. It felt very strange for Squanto to walk where his people once walked. It made him feel lonely to see English homes where Patuxet *wetus* once stood.

Squanto and Samoset brought skins to trade with the English. They also brought some fish.

Squanto learned that the English settlers called themselves Pilgrims. He asked what "pilgrim" meant. They told him a pilgrim was someone who wandered the earth looking for a place to settle.

The Pilgrims explained to Squanto that they had sailed from Plymouth, England. Squanto told them he had once lived in

Plymouth. The Pilgrims told him they were calling their new village Plymouth to honor the place they had sailed from.

Squanto would call the village Plymouth, too. But in his heart, he knew it would always be his Patuxet home.

10
Thank You, Squanto!

Squanto told the Pilgrims that his chief, Massasoit, was nearby. He told them that Massasoit would like to meet with them. The Pilgrims wanted to meet Massasoit. They wanted to trade with the Wampanoags and to be at peace with them.

The Pilgrims sent presents to Massasoit. They sent him two knives and a copper chain with jewels in it. They also sent biscuits and butter. The Pilgrims gave other presents to Massasoit's warriors.

Squanto explained that the Pilgrims came in peace. They wanted Massasoit to come to their village. So Squanto, Massasoit, and sixty warriors went to Plymouth. Before crossing the creek by the village, they set down their bows and arrows to show they came in peace.

The Pilgrims brought out a green rug and three cushions. Massasoit sat down. Squanto told the Pilgrims that Massasoit had come in peace. He told them the Wampanoags wanted to make a peace agreement with the Pilgrims.

The Pilgrims and Massasoit talked for a long time. Squanto was very busy speaking in English, then in the language of his people. Before long, the Wampanoags and the Pilgrims agreed to live side by side as allies.

Squanto was pleased that his people and the Pilgrims had come to an agreement.

The Pilgrims liked Squanto. They asked him if he would stay with them. Squanto said he would.

The Pilgrims needed Squanto's help very much. Squanto saw that the Pilgrims were not good hunters. He taught them how to track deer, bear, raccoons, and squirrels for meat. He showed them how to fish with nets in the streams or with bone fishhooks in the ponds.

He taught them the trick of catching eels by stomping in the mud where they lived. The Pilgrims enjoyed the fat, sweet eels just as Squanto's family had.

When spring came, Squanto was very busy. He showed the Pilgrims the Wampanoag way of planting corn. He remembered how his mother first made a mound of earth. Just like his mother did, Squanto dug a hole in the mound and dropped in three fish. He told the Pilgrims this would make the corn grow better.

Squanto also guided the Pilgrims as they explored the area. He took them to Massasoit's village. He sailed with them around the bay. The Pilgrims met other Native Americans. They traded with them for food and beaver skins.

In the summer, Squanto showed the Pilgrims where to pick the best grapes, strawberries, blueberries, and blackberries. In the fall, Squanto showed them where the cranberries grew red and ripe. He taught the Pilgrims how to cook acorns and how to make acorn cakes. He explained how the Wampanoags dried fish, fruit, and vegetables to eat in the winter.

The Pilgrims listened and learned from Squanto.

That fall, when the harvest was in, the Pilgrims decided to have a special feast. They remembered harvest festivals back in England. They wanted to have a harvest festival in Plymouth. They would give thanks for surviving in this new land. They would give thanks for the excellent harvest that Squanto had helped them to grow.

The Pilgrims sent out hunters. The men returned with ducks, geese, and turkeys. Others caught lobsters and fish. The Pilgrims brought corn, beans, squash, and peas.

To celebrate their friendship with the Wampanoags, the Pilgrims invited Massasoit to their feast. Massasoit came with ninety of his men. They brought five deer to the feast.

The harvest festival lasted for three days.

There was feasting. There were games. There were running and jumping contests. The Pilgrims fired off their guns.

Squanto celebrated, too. The Pilgrims' harvest festival was like his people's harvest celebration with games, dances, and feasting with family and friends. He was thankful his Pilgrim friends had enough food to be able to have a festival.

The Pilgrims were thankful that Squanto was their friend. Without Squanto's skills, knowledge, and friendship, the Pilgrims might not have survived another winter in America.

Squanto's life had been difficult. Twice he had been kidnapped and taken away from his home. Twice he had returned home. Even when he learned that most of his tribe had died, Squanto did not lose faith in himself. He knew he was part of two worlds, his Native American world and the world of the English. By living with and helping the Pilgrims, Squanto brought both worlds together.

Dear Reader,

There are many different ways to tell the story of someone's life. In telling Squanto's story, we followed facts from traditional historical records. We based our book on what we learned about Native American life during this time. We also visited the re-created Wampanoag village, at Plimouth Plantation in Massachusetts, to help us place Squanto within the Native American world in which he grew up.

Happy Reading,
Peter and Connie Roop